THE LAWBOOK EXCHANGE, LTD.
FOUNDATIONS OF THE LAWS OF WAR

GENERAL EDITOR: JOSEPH PERKOVICH

The Foundations of the Laws of War Series presents reprints of works influential in the development of the regulation of armed conflict, humanitarian law, and international criminal law. The reprints feature new scholarly assessments provided by experts in these fields.

INSTRUCTIONS FOR THE GOVERNMENT OF ARMIES OF THE UNITED STATES IN THE FIELD

[WITH]

GUERILLA PARTIES CONSIDERED WITH REFERENCE TO THE LAWS AND USAGES OF WAR

Books in the Series

INSTRUCTIONS

GOVERNMENT OF ARMIES

OF

THE UNITED STATES

IN THE FIELD.

ORIGINALLY ISSUED AS GENERAL ORDERS No. 100,
ADJUTANT GENERAL'S OFFICE, 1863.

GUERRILLA PARTIES

CONSIDERED WITH REFERENCE TO THE

LAWS AND USAGES OF WAR.

WRITTEN AT THE REQUEST OF

MAJOR-GENERAL HENRY W. HALLECK,

GENERAL-IN-CHIEF OF THE ARMY OF THE UNITED STATES.

FRANCIS LIEBER

With a new introduction by
Steve Sheppard
William Enfield Professor of Law,
University of Arkansas School of Law

THE LAWBOOK EXCHANGE, LTD.
Clark, New Jersey

ISBN 9781584775263 (hardcover)
ISBN 9781616191528 (paperback)

Lawbook Exchange edition 2011

The quality of this reprint is equivalent to the quality of the original work.

THE LAWBOOK EXCHANGE, LTD.

33 Terminal Avenue
Clark, New Jersey 07066-1321

*Please see our website for a selection of our other publications
and fine facsimile reprints of classic works of legal history:*
www.lawbookexchange.com

Library of Congress Cataloging-in-Publication Data

Lieber, Francis, 1800-1872.
  Instructions for the government of armies in the United
    States in the field [with] guerilla parties considered with
    reference to the law and usages of war / Francis Lieber ;
    with a new introduction by Steve Sheppard.
      p. cm.
  Originally published: Washington, D.C. : Government Printing
    Office, 1898.
  Includes index.
  ISBN 1-58477-526-2 (alk. paper)
  1. United States. Army--Regulations. 2. Military law--United
  States. I. Title.
KF7221.L54 2005
355.1'33'0973--dc22   2004029673

Printed in the United States of America on acid-free paper

Guerrilla Parties, *The Lieber Code,* and the Law of War

Steve Sheppard

Any reader of Thucydides knows that there have long been limits on the waging of war. For most of human history these limits have been a matter of custom, effectively a series of mutual understandings based on past practice and a sense of the division between the civilized man and the barbarian. The customs of land and maritime warfare that grew out of these understandings informed the various articles of war or standing orders that were issued to fleets and armies. Most of these commands were personal, such as the prohibition on the individual soldier from looting or theft. The broader limits on the conduct of war, the whole of *jus in bello,* remained uncodified and were, largely, discretionary with commanders in the field.

This state of affairs was bound to change somewhere between the time of Cromwell's New Model Army and the end of the nineteenth century. These three centuries saw transitions from the exclusive of use of professional armies to the *levée en masse,* an enormous increase in the size of battlefields, exponential growth in the number of civilians brought into contact with the front, and the development of more powerful weapons, which increased the amount of collateral death and destruction. Over the course of this period the need to reconcile the effect of these developments with

i

accepted norms became a matter of ever greater concern, both for professional soldiers and civilian officials.

This reconciliation was accomplished by a Prussian immigrant, a man of letters and scholar of Roman law who became a student and champion of American institutions and raised immigrant companies for the Union army, even while one of his sons fought and died for the Confederacy. Francis Lieber, a professor at Columbia Law School in New York, fought as a young infantryman at the Battle of Waterloo before becoming a revolutionary, scholar, and political scientist. He had taught in England and South Carolina before his move to New York, and his acquaintances included most of the leading intellectuals of the North and the South. At the beginning of the war he was already well known in his adopted United States as a legal scholar and political scientist, and as the creator of the *Encyclopedia Americana*, which was largely translated from the great German Brockhaus encyclopedia and supplemented with original entries relating to the United States by himself and his American allies in various fields, such as Joseph Story in law.

As the war progressed Lieber grew increasingly concerned that Union troops lacked sufficient training in the laws of war. This topic had long fascinated the former soldier. Indeed, it was an important theme in his 1838 study, *A Manual of Political Ethics*. This was a matter of grave concern, he reasoned, in a war fought largely by volunteers who lacked training in a professional culture of arms, and who were encountering an increasing numbers of problems in their dealings with prisoners and civilians. In February 1862, Hamilton, one of Lieber's three sons in uniform, was wounded in the western campaign near Fort Donelson, Tennessee. Lieber visited him during his convalescence and met the departmental commander, General Henry Halleck. Halleck, a lawyer by training, was the author of *International Law, or Rules Regulating the Intercourse of States in Peace and War* (1861). Their conversation was the catalyst for the two pamphlets reproduced in this edition. Although Lieber conceived of writing a "little book on the law of war" for army use as early as 1861, it was this encounter that inspired him to commit his thoughts to paper.

In a letter written in August 1862 Halleck asked Lieber to offer his opinion to the public about the war's most vexing question concerning the rules of engagement thus far: the identification and treatment of irregulars. Halleck complained that the Confederate authorities claimed "the right to send men, in the garb of peaceful citizens," to attack troops and property behind the lines, but demanded that they "be treated as ordinary belligerents" if caught. Further, Halleck noted that the Confederates "threaten that if such persons be punished as marauders and spies, they will retaliate by executing our prisoners in their possession."[1]

Lieber's response, *Guerrilla Parties Considered with Reference to the Laws and Usages of War*, was completed only weeks after Halleck's request. The pamphlet, the second title in this reprint edition, is a narrative rather than a set of instructions. Lieber first considers the meaning of the "guerrilla" and develops not only a definition of the term but a

---

[1] *Guerilla Parties*, 3.

history of the difficulties in assessing the legal responsibilities owed by them and to them by regular soldiers. His definition has a very current ring to it. " [A] guerrilla party means an irregular band of armed men, carrying on an irregular war, not being able, according to their character as a guerrilla party to carry on what the law terms a *regular* war."[2] In other words, they were distinguished from a regular army by the irregularity of their origin and the nature of their command, pay, structure, and continuity. He unpacked this concept into a variety of forms distinct from guerrilla parties generally. One example is the war-rebel, who organizes resistance against a victorious and occupying army. Unless such a party is a component of a true national uprising against this force, he reasoned, that party should be summarily executed unless pardoned on prudential grounds.

One of the most important contributions of Lieber's *Consideration* ran against Halleck's apparent desire. Lieber was unwilling to strip guerrillas of the protection of the law of war for their failure to fight in uniform. This question was critical to commanders in the field as well as to Halleck, and it remains the essence of the law of war: what conduct and appearance in a combatant is sufficient to accrue protection by the laws of war (non-combatants being protected already)? Rather than the bright-line test of uniform that Halleck then seems to have favored, Lieber gave a careful, judicious answer based on the intent of the soldier; clothing alone did not make the difference, only the intent to deceive. Guerrillas aiding the main force of

---

[2] *Ibid.,* 7.

a belligerent army captured without uniforms in fair and open fighting should be treated as prisoners of war, small bands of prowlers and bushwackers who take it on themselves to harass an army opposing their state should not. Halleck, then general-in-chief of the army of the United States, was pleased with the effort and ordered 5,000 copies printed and distributed to units in the field. These quickly made their ways to Confederate hands, and the pamphlet was apparently influential on both sides.

Halleck sought immediately to expand the effort of enunciating the legal principles that applied to the American conflict. Through his influence in December 1862, Lieber was the sole civilian appointed to a panel enlisted to create a code of regulations for the armies in the field. The other members of the committee were experienced senior officers with legal, educational, and administrative backgrounds. Major General George Cadwalader and Brigadier General J.H. Martindale were lawyers of some renown. Major General George L. Hartsuff was a West Point instructor. Major General Ethan Allen Hitchcock, a legend of the Seminole and Mexican Wars, was an expert on military administration.

With their assistance Lieber drafted a code based on a rich survey of military customs and practices. From this, Lieber reduced rules that were guided by his deep sense that a soldier is never freed from ethical obligations, but leavened with his understanding of the dictates of combat. The resulting document outlined a comprehensive list of carefully defined rules regarding the protection of non-combatants, the acceptance of prisoners, and limits on the unnecessary use of force that were clear in their obligations and their rationales, but flexible enough to apply to specific situations in the field. The rules governing the treatment of prisoners would be amplified by a further pamphlet Lieber would write in 1865, but the outlines were established clearly in this earlier work. The most controversial aspects of the code, and those that have been least followed in later law, reflected Lieber's willingness to allow commanders to contravene even the strictest obligations, allowing them exceptions in cases of necessity and retaliation. Despite the repudiation of a general exception, the principle Lieber enunciated continues to have influence, that military necessity permits the "direct destruction of life or limb of *armed* enemies, and of other persons whose destruction is incidentally *unavoidable*."[3]

In February 1863 Lieber presented his draft to the committee. It was then printed with wide margins and distributed for comment. Not waiting for the committee, Halleck moved ahead on one portion of the draft, issuing the sections on prisoner exchange and parol as General Orders Number 49, on February 29, 1863. Halleck and the committee made several changes, most importantly asking Lieber to add what became, after Lieber's drafting and some judicious editing by Halleck himself, Section Ten, which deals with civil war and insurrection. Lieber later took great pride in the final draft and, although it reflected the work of Halleck and the committee, endorsed it wholeheartedly in later years.

---

[3] *Instructions for the Government of the Armies*, 7.

The final document was approved by Secretary of War Stanton and President Lincoln, authorized by the Adjutant General in April, and issued in May 1863 as General Orders 100. It was distributed immediately to officers in the field and also sent to the government and armies of the Confederacy. The orders were followed and cited, by and large, by both sides. The U.S. Supreme Court applied it in occupation and reconstruction cases, and it remained the basis of U.S. Army policy throughout the nineteenth century. Indeed, the edition reproduced here was printed by the Adjutant General in 1898 for use by forces in the Spanish-American War. Its text is unaltered from its 1863 printing.[4] Indeed, FM 27-10, the current U.S. Army manual on the law of land warfare, which was modified only slightly since the Korean War version replaced the 1940 edition, owes much to its 1863 grandfather.

The influence on international law of General Orders 100 or, as it quickly became known abroad, the Lieber Code, was profound. Although only a national code, it inspired similar codes for the great continental military powers and served as a foundation of the international treaties considered at the Brussels Conference of 1874 that were adopted in the Hague Conventions of 1899 and 1907, which in turn influenced the Geneva conventions and later protocols. From these conventions followed further international agreements, including not only the conferences in

---

[4] The present volume reprints the 1898 edition rather than the 1863 edition, which it fully restates without amendment. We have offered the later printing, as it is in a larger format with a more legible typeface.

vii

Geneva, but also the trials in Nuremburg and Tokyo following the Second World War. At the close of the twentieth century, the law of war as captured by Lieber was a clear influence on the Rome Treaty, which finally established an International Criminal Court for the prosecution of war crimes in 1998.

Thus, in the space of a century and a half, the customs of war had moved from the rough approximations of past practices into a codified series of specific obligation that extended beyond purely disciplinary matters within ranks, subject to the vagaries of commanders and national will for enforcement, to the realm of international obligations. Moreover, these obligations, just as Lieber required, were not upon armies and states but upon the individual soldiers and sailors, whose ethical obligations to limit the harm they cause to a reasoned minimum has become the basis for individual accountability, increasingly among vanquished and victor alike. As with all laws, there is no perfection in enforcement, but there is a greater worldwide obedience than observers often credit. From the start given in General Orders 100, the law has grown globally, such that the brutality and horrors of war have been, at least slightly, reduced.

Further Reading

Carnahan, Burrus M. "Lincoln, Lieber and the Laws of War: the Origins and Limits of the Principle of Military Necessity." *American Journal of International Law* (1998): 92 p. 213.

Carrington, Paul D. "A Tale of Two Lawyers." *Northwestern University Law Review* (1997): 91 p. 615.

Davis, George B. "Doctor Francis Lieber's Instructions for the Government of Armies in the Field." *American Journal of International Law* (1907): 1, p. 13.

Doty, Grant R. "The United States and the Development of the Laws of Land Warfare." *Military Law Review* (1998): 156, p. 224

Freidel, Frank. *Francis Lieber: Nineteenth-Century Liberal*. Baton Rouge: Louisiana State University Press, 1947 (Lawbook Exchange, 2003).

Hartigan, Richard Shelly, *Lieber's Code & the Law of War*. Chicago, Illinois: Precedent Publishing, Inc., 1983.

Hoeflich, Michael. "Roman and Civil Law in American Legal Education and Research Prior to 1930: A Preliminary Survey." *University of Illinois Law Review* (1984), p. 719.

Hoeflich, Michael H. *Roman and Civil Law and the Development of Anglo-American Jurisprudence in the Nineteenth Century.* Athens: University of Georgia Press, 1997.

"A Lieber Bibliography, with Annotations." *Cardozo Law Review* (1995): 16, p. 2321

Lieber, Francis. *Manual of Political Ethics, Designed Chiefly for the Use of Colleges and Students at Law.* (Second Edition, Revised. Edited by Theodore D. Woolsey) Philadelphia: J.B. Lippincott Company, 1890 (Lawbook Exchange, 2003).

Lieber, Francis, *Miscellaneous Writings.* Philadelphia: J.B. Lippincott & Co., 1881 (Lawbook Exchange, 2003) (volume two contains "1863 General Orders 100," "On Guerrilla Parties" and "On Prisoners of War").

Meron, Theodor. "Francis Lieber's Code and Principles of Humanity." *Columbia Journal of Transnational Law* (1997): 36, p. 269

Morris, Scott R. "The Laws of War: Rules by Warriors for Warriors." *Army Lawyer* (1997), p. 4.

United States Department of the Army, Field Manual 27-10, *The Law of Land Warfare.* 18 July 1956 (rev'd 15 July 1976).

INSTRUCTIONS

FOR THE

GOVERNMENT OF ARMIES

OF

THE UNITED STATES

IN THE FIELD.

PREPARED BY

FRANCIS LIEBER, LL.D.

ORIGINALLY ISSUED AS GENERAL ORDERS No. 100,
ADJUTANT GENERAL'S OFFICE, 1863.

WASHINGTON:
GOVERNMENT PRINTING OFFICE.
1898.

GENERAL ORDERS,
No. 100.

WAR DEPARTMENT,
ADJUTANT GENERAL'S OFFICE,
Washington, April 24, 1863.

The following "Instructions for the Government of Armies of the United States in the Field," prepared by FRANCIS LIEBER, LL.D., and revised by a Board of Officers, of which Major General E. A. HITCHCOCK is president, having been approved by the President of the United States, he commands that they be published for the information of all concerned.

BY ORDER OF THE SECRETARY OF WAR:

E. D. TOWNSEND,
Assistant Adjutant General.

INSTRUCTIONS FOR THE GOVERNMENT OF ARMIES OF THE UNITED STATES IN THE FIELD.

SECTION I.

Martial law—Military jurisdiction—Military necessity—Retaliation.

1.

A place, district, or country occupied by an enemy stands, in consequence of the occupation, under the Martial Law of the invading or occupying army, whether any proclamation declaring Martial Law, or any public warning to the inhabitants, has been issued or not. Martial Law is the immediate and direct effect and consequence of occupation or conquest.

The presence of a hostile army proclaims its Martial Law.

2.

Martial Law does not cease during the hostile occupation, except by special proclamation, ordered by the commander in chief; or by special mention in the treaty of peace concluding the war, when the occupation of a place or territory continues beyond the conclusion of peace as one of the conditions of the same.

3.

Martial Law in a hostile country consists in the suspension, by the occupying military authority, of the criminal and civil law, and of the domestic administration and government in the occupied place or territory, and in the substitution of military rule and force for the same, as well as in the dictation of general laws, as far as military necessity requires this suspension, substitution, or dictation.

The commander of the forces may proclaim that the administration of all civil and penal law shall continue either wholly or in part, as in times of peace, unless otherwise ordered by the military authority.

4.

Martial Law is simply military authority exercised in accordance with the laws and usages of war. Military oppression is not Martial Law; it is the abuse of the power which that law confers. As Martial Law is executed by military force, it is incumbent upon those who administer it to be strictly guided by the principles of justice, honor, and humanity—virtues adorning a soldier even more than other men, for the very reason that he possesses the power of his arms against the unarmed.

5.

Martial Law should be less stringent in places and countries fully occupied and fairly conquered. Much greater severity may be exercised in places or regions where actual hostilities exist, or are expected and must be prepared for. Its most complete sway is allowed—even in the commander's own country—when face to face with the enemy, because of the absolute necessities of the case, and of the paramount duty to defend the country against invasion.

To save the country is paramount to all other considerations.

6.

All civil and penal law shall continue to take its usual course in the enemy's places and territories under Martial Law, unless interrupted or stopped by order of the occupying military power; but all the functions of the hostile government—legislative, executive, or administrative—whether of a general, provincial, or local character, cease under Martial Law, or continue only with the sanction, or, if deemed necessary, the participation of the occupier or invader.

7.

Martial Law extends to property, and to persons, whether they are subjects of the enemy or aliens to that government.

8.

Consuls, among American and European nations, are not diplomatic agents. Nevertheless, their offices and persons will be subjected to Martial Law in cases of urgent necessity only: their property and business are not exempted. Any delinquency they commit against the established military rule may be punished as in the case of any other inhabitant, and such punishment furnishes no reasonable ground for international complaint.

9.

The functions of Ambassadors, Ministers, or other diplomatic agents, accredited by neutral powers to the hostile government, cease, so far as regards the displaced government; but the conquering or occupying power usually recognizes them as temporarily accredited to itself.

10.

Martial Law affects chiefly the police and collection of public revenue and taxes, whether imposed by the expelled government or by the invader, and refers mainly to the support and efficiency of the army, its safety, and the safety of its operations.

11.

The law of war does not only disclaim all cruelty and bad faith concerning engagements concluded with the enemy during the war, but also the breaking of stipulations solemnly contracted by the belligerents in time of peace, and avowedly intended to remain in force in case of war between the contracting powers.

It disclaims all extortions and other transactions for individual gain; all acts of private revenge, or connivance at such acts.

Offenses to the contrary shall be severely punished, and especially so if committed by officers.

12.

Whenever feasible, Martial Law is carried out in cases of individual offenders by Military Courts; but sentences of death shall be executed only with the approval of the chief executive, provided the urgency of the case does not require a speedier execution, and then only with the approval of the chief commander.

13.

Military jurisdiction is of two kinds: First, that which is conferred and defined by statute; second, that which is derived from the common law of war. Military offenses under the statute law must be tried in the manner therein directed; but military offenses which do not come within the statute must be tried and punished under the common law of war. The character of the courts which exercise these jurisdictions depends upon the local laws of each particular country.

In the armies of the United States the first is exercised by courts-martial, while cases which do not come within the "Rules and Articles of War," or the jurisdiction conferred by statute on courts-martial, are tried by military commissions.

14.

Military necessity, as understood by modern civilized nations, consists in the necessity of those measures which are indispensable for securing the ends of the war, and which are lawful according to the modern law and usages of war.

15.

Military necessity admits of all direct destruction of life or limb of *armed* enemies, and of other persons whose destruction is incidentally *unavoidable* in the armed contests of the war; it allows of the capturing of every armed enemy, and every enemy of importance to the hostile government, or of peculiar danger to the captor; it allows of all destruction of property, and obstruction of the ways and channels of traffic, travel, or communication, and of all withholding of sustenance or means of life from the enemy; of the appropriation of whatever an enemy's country affords necessary for the subsistence and safety of the army, and of such deception as does not involve the breaking of good faith either positively pledged, regarding agreements entered into during the war, or supposed by the modern law of war to exist. Men who take up arms against one another in public war do not cease on this account to be moral beings, responsible to one another and to God.

16.

Military necessity does not admit of cruelty—that is, the infliction of suffering for the sake of suffering or for revenge, nor of maiming or wounding except in fight, nor of torture to extort confessions. It does not admit of the use of poison in any way, nor of the wanton devastation of a district. It admits of deception, but disclaims acts of perfidy; and, in general, military necessity does not include any act of hostility which makes the return to peace unnecessarily difficult.

17.

War is not carried on by arms alone. It is lawful to starve the hostile belligerent, armed or unarmed, so that it leads to the speedier subjection of the enemy.

18.

When a commander of a besieged place expels the noncombatants, in order to lessen the number of those who consume his stock of provisions, it is lawful, though an extreme measure, to drive them back, so as to hasten on the surrender.

19.

Commanders, whenever admissible, inform the enemy of their intention to bombard a place, so that the noncombatants, and especially the women and children, may be removed before the bombardment commences. But it is no infraction of the common law of war to omit thus to inform the enemy. Surprise may be a necessity.

20.

Public war is a state of armed hostility between sovereign nations or governments. It is a law and requisite of civilized existence that men live in political, continuous societies, forming organized units, called states or nations, whose constituents bear, enjoy, and, suffer, advance and retrograde together, in peace and in war.

21.

The citizen or native of a hostile country is thus an enemy, as one of the constituents of the hostile state or nation, and as such is subjected to the hardships of the war.

22.

Nevertheless, as civilization has advanced during the last centuries, so has likewise steadily advanced, especially in war on land, the distinction between the private individual belonging to a hostile country and the hostile country itself, with its men in arms. The principle has been more and more acknowledged that the unarmed citizen is to be spared in person, property, and honor as much as the exigencies of war will admit.

23.

Private citizens are no longer murdered, enslaved, or carried off to distant parts, and the inoffensive individual is as little disturbed in his private relations as the commander of the hostile troops can afford to grant in the overruling demands of a vigorous war.

24.

The almost universal rule in remote times was, and continues to be with barbarous armies, that the private individual of the hostile country is destined to suffer every privation of liberty and protection, and every disruption of family ties. Protection was, and still is with uncivilized people, the exception.

25.

In modern regular wars of the Europeans, and their descendants in other portions of the globe, protection of the inoffensive citizen of the hostile country is the rule; privation and disturbance of private relations are the exceptions.

26.

Commanding generals may cause the magistrates and civil officers of the hostile country to take the oath of temporary allegiance or an oath of fidelity to their own victorious government or rulers, and they may expel every one who declines to do so. But whether they do so or not, the people and their civil officers owe strict obedience to them as long as they hold sway over the district or country, at the peril of their lives.

27.

The law of war can no more wholly dispense with retaliation than can the law of nations, of which it is a branch. Yet civilized nations acknowledge retaliation as the sternest feature of war. A reckless enemy often leaves to his opponent no other means of securing himself against the repetition of barbarous outrage.

28.

Retaliation will, therefore, never be resorted to as a measure of mere revenge, but only as a means of protective retribution, and moreover, cautiously and unavoidably; that is to say, retaliation shall only be resorted to after careful inquiry into the real occurrence, and the character of the misdeeds that may demand retribution.

Unjust or inconsiderate retaliation removes the belligerents farther and farther from the mitigating rules of regular war, and by rapid steps leads them nearer to the internecine wars of savages.

29.

Modern times are distinguished from earlier ages by the existence, at one and the same time, of many nations and great governments related to one another in close intercourse.

Peace is their normal condition; war is the exception. The ultimate object of all modern war is a renewed state of peace.

The more vigorously wars are pursued, the better it is for humanity. Sharp wars are brief.

30.

Every since the formation and coexistence of modern nations, and ever since wars have become great national wars, war has come to be acknowledged not to be its own end, but the means to obtain great ends of state, or to consist in defense against wrong; and no conventional restriction of the modes adopted to injure the enemy is any longer admitted; but the law of war imposes many limitations and restrictions on principles of justice, faith, and honor.

SECTION II.

Public and private property of the enemy—Protection of persons, and especially of women; of religion, the arts and sciences—Punishment of crimes against the inhabitants of hostile countries.

31.

A victorious army appropriates all public money, seizes all public movable property until further direction by its government, and sequesters for its own benefit or of that of its government all the revenues of real property belonging to the hostile government or nation. The title to such real property remains in abeyance during military occupation, and until the conquest is made complete.

32.

A victorious army, by the martial power inherent in the same, may suspend, change, or abolish, as far as the martial power extends, the relations which arise from the services due, according to the existing laws of the invaded country, from one citizen, subject, or native of the same to another.

The commander of the army must leave it to the ultimate treaty of peace to settle the permanency of this change.

33.

It is no longer considered lawful—on the contrary, it is held to be a serious breach of the law of war—to force the subjects of the enemy into the service of the victorious government, except the latter should proclaim, after a fair and complete conquest of the hostile country or district, that it is resolved to keep the country, district, or place permanently as its own and make it a portion of its own country.

34.

As a general rule, the property belonging to churches, to hospitals, or other establishments of an exclusively charitable character, to establishments of education, or foundations for the promotion of knowledge, whether public schools, universities, academies of learning or observatories, museums of the fine arts, or of a scientific character—such property is not to be considered public property in the sense of paragraph 31; but it may be taxed or used when the public service may require it.

35.

Classical works of art, libraries, scientific collections, or precious instruments, such as astronomical telescopes, as well as hospitals, must be secured against all avoidable injury, even when they are contained in fortified places whilst besieged or bombarded.

36.

If such works of art, libraries, collections, or instruments belonging to a hostile nation or government, can be removed without injury, the ruler of the conquering state or nation may order them to be seized and removed for the benefit of the said nation. The ultimate ownership is to be settled by the ensuing treaty of peace.

In no case shall they be sold or given away, if captured by the armies of the United States, nor shall they ever be privately appropriated, or wantonly destroyed or injured.

37.

The United States acknowledge and protect, in hostile countries occupied by them, religion and morality; strictly private property; the persons of the inhabitants, especially those of women; and the sacredness of domestic relations. Offenses to the contrary shall be rigorously punished.

This rule does not interfere with the right of the victorious invader to tax the people or their property, to levy forced loans, to billet soldiers, or to appropriate property, especially houses, lands, boats or ships, and churches, for temporary and military uses.

38.

Private property, unless forfeited by crimes or by offenses of the owner, can be seized only by way of military necessity, for the support or other benefit of the army or of the United States.

If the owner has not fled, the commanding officer will cause receipts to be given, which may serve the spoliated owner to obtain indemnity.

39.

The salaries of civil officers of the hostile government who remain in the invaded territory, and continue the work of their office, and can continue it according to the circumstances arising out of the war—such as judges, administrative or police officers, officers of city or communal governments—

are paid from the public revenue of the invaded territory, until the military government has reason wholly or partially to discontinue it. Salaries or incomes connected with purely honorary titles are always stopped.

40.

There exists no law or body of authoritative rules of action between hostile armies, except that branch of the law of nature and nations which is called the law and usages of war on land.

41.

All municipal law of the ground on which the armies stand, or of the countries to which they belong, is silent and of no effect between armies in the field.

42.

Slavery, complicating and confounding the ideas of property, (that is of a *thing*,) and of personality, (that is of *humanity*,) exists according to municipal or local law only. The law of nature and nations has never acknowledged it. The digest of the Roman law enacts the early dictum of the pagan jurist, that "so far as the law of nature is concerned, all men are equal." Fugitives escaping from a country in which they were slaves, villains, or serfs, into another country, have, for centuries past, been held free and acknowledged free by judicial decisions of European countries, even though the municipal law of the country in which the slave had taken refuge acknowledged slavery within its own dominions.

43.

Therefore, in a war between the United States and a belligerent which admits of slavery, if a person held in bondage by that belligerent be captured by or come as a fugitive under the protection of the military forces of the United States, such person is immediately entitled to the rights and privileges of a freeman. To return such person into slavery would amount to enslaving a free person, and neither the United States nor any officer under their authority can enslave any human being. Moreover, a person so made free by the law of war is under the shield of the law of nations, and the former owner or State can have, by the law of postliminy, no belligerent lien or claim of service.

44.

All wanton violence committed against persons in the invaded country, all destruction of property not commanded by the authorized officer, all robbery, all pillage or sacking, even after taking a place by main force, all rape, wounding, maiming, or killing of such inhabitants, are prohibited under the penalty of death, or such other severe punishment as may seem adequate for the gravity of the offense.

A soldier, officer or private, in the act of committing such violence, and disobeying a superior ordering him to abstain from it, may be lawfully killed on the spot by such superior.

45.

All captures and booty belong, according to the modern law of war, primarily to the government of the captor.

Prize money, whether on sea or land, can now only be claimed under local law.

46.

Neither officers nor soldiers are allowed to make use of their position or power in the hostile country for private gain, not even for commercial transactions otherwise legitimate. Offenses to the contrary committed by commissioned officers will be punished with cashiering or such other punishment as the nature of the offense may require; if by soldiers, they shall be punished according to the nature of the offense.

47.

Crimes punishable by all penal codes, such as arson, murder, maiming, assaults, highway robbery, theft, burglary, fraud, forgery, and rape, if committed by an American soldier in a hostile country against its inhabitants, are not only punishable as at home, but in all cases in which death is not inflicted, the severer punishment shall be preferred.

SECTION III.

Deserters—Prisoners of war—Hostages—Booty on the battle-field.

48.

Deserters from the American Army, having entered the service of the enemy, suffer death if they fall again into the hands of the United States, whether by capture, or being delivered up to the American Army; and if a deserter from the enemy, having taken service in the Army of the United

1115——2

States, is captured by the enemy, and punished by them with death or otherwise, it is not a breach against the law and usages of war, requiring redress or retaliation.

49.

A prisoner of war is a public enemy armed or attached to the hostile army for active aid, who has fallen into the hands of the captor, either fighting or wounded, on the field or in the hospital, by individual surrender or by capitulation.

All soldiers, of whatever species of arms; all men who belong to the rising *en masse* of the hostile country; all those who are attached to the army for its efficiency and promote directly the object of the war, except such as are hereinafter provided for; all disabled men or officers on the field or elsewhere, if captured; all enemies who have thrown away their arms and ask for quarter, are prisoners of war, and as such exposed to the inconveniences as well as entitled to the privileges of a prisoner of war.

50.

Moreover, citizens who accompany an army for whatever purpose, such as sutlers, editors, or reporters of journals, or contractors, if captured, may be made prisoners of war, and be detained as such.

The monarch and members of the hostile reigning family, male or female, the chief, and chief officers of the hostile government, its diplomatic agents, and all persons who are of particular and singular use and benefit to the hostile army or its government, are, if captured on belligerent ground, and if unprovided with a safe conduct granted by the captor's government, prisoners of war.

51.

If the people of that portion of an invaded country which is not yet occupied by the enemy, or of the whole country, at the approach of a hostile army, rise, under a duly authorized levy, *en masse* to resist the invader, they are now treated as public enemies, and, if captured, are prisoners of war.

52.

No belligerent has the right to declare that he will treat every captured man in arms of a levy *en masse* as a brigand or bandit.

If, however, the people of a country, or any portion of the same, already occupied by an army, rise against it, they are violators of the laws of war, and are not entitled to their protection.

53.

The enemy's chaplains, officers of the medical staff, apothecaries, hospital nurses and servants, if they fall into the hands of the American Army, are not prisoners of war, unless the commander has reasons to retain them. In this latter case, or if, at their own desire, they are allowed to remain with their captured companions, they are treated as prisoners of war, and may be exchanged if the commander sees fit.

54.

A hostage is a person accepted as a pledge for the fulfillment of an agreement concluded between belligerents during the war, or in consequence of a war. Hostages are rare in the present age.

55.

If a hostage is accepted, he is treated like a prisoner of war, according to rank and condition, as circumstances may admit.

56.

A prisoner of war is subject to no punishment for being a public enemy, nor is any revenge wreaked upon him by the intentional infliction of any suffering, or disgrace, by cruel imprisonment, want of food, by mutilation, death, or any other barbarity.

57.

So soon as a man is armed by a sovereign government and takes the soldier's oath of fidelity, he is a belligerent; his killing, wounding, or other warlike acts are not individual crimes or offenses. No belligerent has a right to declare that enemies of a certain class, color, or condition, when properly organized as soldiers, will not be treated by him as public enemies.

58.

The law of nations knows of no distinction of color, and if an enemy of the United States should enslave and sell any captured persons of their army, it would be a case for the severest retaliation, if not redressed upon complaint.

The United States can not retaliate by enslavement; therefore death must be the retaliation for this crime against the law of nations.

59.

A prisoner of war remains answerable for his crimes committed against the captor's army or people, committed before he was captured, and for which he has not been punished by his own authorities.

All prisoners of war are liable to the infliction of retaliatory measures.

60.

It is against the usage of modern war to resolve, in hatred and revenge, to give no quarter. No body of troops has the right to declare that it will not give, and therefore will not expect, quarter; but a commander is permitted to direct his troops to give no quarter, in great straits, when his own salvation makes it *impossible* to cumber himself with prisoners.

61.

Troops that give no quarter have no right to kill enemies already disabled on the ground, or prisoners captured by other troops.

62.

All troops of the enemy known or discovered to give no quarter in general, or to any portion of the army, receive none.

63.

Troops who fight in the uniform of their enemies, without any plain, striking, and uniform mark of distinction of their own, can expect no quarter.

64.

If American troops capture a train containing uniforms of the enemy, and the commander considers it advisable to distribute them for use among his men, some striking mark or sign must be adopted to distinguish the American soldier from the enemy.

65.

The use of the enemy's national standard, flag, or other emblem of nationality, for the purpose of deceiving the enemy in battle, is an act of perfidy by which they lose all claim to the protection of the laws of war.

66.

Quarter having been given to an enemy by American troops, under a misapprehension of his true character, he may, nevertheless, be ordered to suffer death if, within three days after the battle, it be discovered that he belongs to a corps which gives no quarter.

67.

The law of nations allows every sovereign government to make war upon another sovereign state, and, therefore, admits of no rules or laws different from those of regular warfare, regarding the treatment of prisoners of war, although they may belong to the army of a government which the captor may consider as a wanton and unjust assailant.

68.

Modern wars are not internecine wars, in which the killing of the enemy is the object. The destruction of the enemy in modern war, and, indeed, modern war itself, are means to obtain that object of the belligerent which lies beyond the war.

Unnecessary or revengeful destruction of life is not lawful.

69.

Outposts, sentinels, or pickets are not to be fired upon, except to drive them in, or when a positive order, special or general, has been issued to that effect.

70.

The use of poison in any manner, be it to poison wells, or food, or arms, is wholly excluded from modern warfare. He that uses it puts himself out of the pale of the law and usages of war.

71.

Whoever intentionally inflicts additional wounds on an enemy already wholly disabled, or kills such an enemy, or who orders or encourages soldiers to do so, shall suffer death, if duly convicted, whether he belongs to the Army of the United States, or is an enemy captured after having committed his misdeed.

72.

Money and other valuables on the person of a prisoner, such as watches or jewelry, as well as extra clothing, are regarded by the American Army as the private property of the prisoner, and the appropriation of such valuables or money is considered dishonorable, and is prohibited.

Nevertheless, if *large* sums are found upon the persons of prisoners, or in their possession, they shall be taken from them, and the surplus, after providing for their own support, appropriated for the use of the army, under the direction of the commander, unless otherwise ordered by the government. Nor can prisoners claim, as private property, large sums found and captured in their train, although they have been placed in the private luggage of the prisoners.

73.

All officers, when captured, must surrender their side arms to the captor. They may be restored to the prisoner in marked cases, by the commander, to signalize admiration of his distinguished bravery or approbation of his humane treatment of prisoners before his capture. The captured officer to whom they may be restored can not wear them during captivity.

74.

A prisoner of war, being a public enemy, is the prisoner of the government, and not of the captor. No ransom can be paid by a prisoner of war to his individual captor or to any officer in command. The government alone releases captives, according to rules prescribed by itself.

75.

Prisoners of war are subject to confinement or imprisonment such as may be deemed necessary on account of safety, but they are to be subjected to no other intentional suffering or indignity. The confinement and mode of treating a prisoner may be varied during his captivity according to the demands of safety.

76.

Prisoners of war shall be fed upon plain and wholesome food, whenever practicable, and treated with humanity.

They may be required to work for the benefit of the captor's government, according to their rank and condition.

77.

A prisoner of war who escapes may be shot or otherwise killed in his flight; but neither death nor any other punishment shall be inflicted upon him simply for his attempt to escape, which the law of war does not consider a crime. Stricter means of security shall be used after an unsuccessful attempt at escape.

If, however, a conspiracy is discovered, the purpose of which is a united or general escape, the conspirators may be rigorously punished, even with death; and capital punishment may also be inflicted upon prisoners of war discovered to have plotted rebellion against the authorities of the captors, whether in union with fellow prisoners or other persons.

78.

If prisoners of war, having given no pledge nor made any promise on their honor, forcibly or otherwise escape, and are captured again in battle after having rejoined their own army, they shall not be punished for their escape, but shall be treated as simple prisoners of war, although they will be subjected to stricter confinement.

79.

Every captured wounded enemy shall be medically treated, according to the ability of the medical staff.

80.

Honorable men, when captured, will abstain from giving to the enemy information concerning their own army, and the modern law of war permits no longer the use of any violence against prisoners in order to extort the desired information or to punish them for having given false information.

SECTION IV.

Partisans—Armed enemies not belonging to the hostile army— Scouts—Armed prowlers—War-rebels.

81.

Partisans are soldiers armed and wearing the uniform of their army, but belonging to a corps which acts detached from the main body for the purpose of making inroads into the territory occupied by the enemy. If captured, they are entitled to all the privileges of the prisoner of war.

82.

Men, or squads of men, who commit hostilities, whether by fighting, or inroads for destruction or plunder, or by raids of any kind, without commission, without being part and portion of the organized hostile army, and without sharing continuously in the war, but who do so with intermitting returns to their homes and avocations, or with the occasional assumption of the semblance of peaceful pursuits, divesting themselves of the character or appearance of soldiers—such men, or squads of men, are not public enemies, and, therefore, if captured, are not entitled to the privileges of prisoners of war, but shall be treated summarily as highway robbers or pirates.

83.

Scouts, or single soldiers, if disguised in the dress of the country or in the uniform of the army hostile to their own, employed in obtaining information, if found within or lurking about the lines of the captor, are treated as spies, and suffer death.

84.

Armed prowlers, by whatever names they may be called, or persons of the enemy's territory, who steal within the lines of the hostile army for the purpose of robbing, killing, or of destroying bridges, roads, or canals, or of robbing or destroying the mail, or of cutting the telegraph wires, are not entitled to the privileges of the prisoner of war.

85.

War-rebels are persons within an occupied territory who rise in arms against the occupying or conquering army, or against the authorities established by the same. If captured, they may suffer death, whether they rise singly, in small or large bands, and whether called upon to do so by their own, but expelled, government or not. They are not prisoners of war; nor are they if discovered and secured before their conspiracy has matured to an actual rising or armed violence.

SECTION V.

Safe-conduct—Spies—War-traitors—Captured messengers—Abuse of the flag of truce.

86.

All intercourse between the territories occupied by belligerent armies, whether by traffic, by letter, by travel, or in any other way, ceases. This is the general rule, to be observed without special proclamation.

Exceptions to this rule, whether by safe-conduct, or permission to trade on a small or large scale, or by exchanging mails, or by travel from one territory into the other, can take place only according to agreement approved by the government, or by the highest military authority.

Contraventions of this rule are highly punishable.

87.

Ambassadors, and all other diplomatic agents of neutral powers, accredited to the enemy, may receive safe-conducts through the territories occupied by the belligerents, unless there are military reasons to the contrary, and unless they may reach the place of their destination conveniently by another route. It implies no international affront if the safe-conduct is declined. Such passes are usually given by the supreme authority of the State, and not by subordinate officers.

88.

A spy is a person who secretly, in disguise or under false pretense, seeks information with the intention of communicating it to the enemy.

The spy is punishable with death by hanging by the neck, whether or not he succeed in obtaining the information or in conveying it to the enemy.

89.

If a citizen of the United States obtains information in a legitimate manner, and betrays it to the enemy, be he a military or civil officer, or a private citizen, he shall suffer death.

90.

A traitor under the law of war, or a war-traitor, is a person in a place or district under martial law who, unauthorized by the military commander, gives information of any kind to the enemy, or holds intercourse with him.

91.

The war-traitor is always severely punished. If his offense consists in betraying to the enemy anything concerning the condition, safety, operations, or plans of the troops holding or occupying the place or district, his punishment is death.

92.

If the citizen or subject of a country or place invaded or conquered gives information to his own government, from which he is separated by the hostile army, or to the army of his government, he is a war-traitor, and death is the penalty of his offense.

93.

All armies in the field stand in need of guides, and impress them if they can not obtain them otherwise.

94.

No person having been forced by the enemy to serve as guide is punishable for having done so.

95.

If a citizen of a hostile and invaded district voluntarily serves as a guide to the enemy, or offers to do so, he is deemed a war-traitor, and shall suffer death.

96.

A citizen serving voluntarily as a guide against his own country commits treason, and will be dealt with according to the law of his country.

97.

Guides, when it is clearly proved that they have misled intentionally, may be put to death.

98.

All unauthorized or secret communication with the enemy is considered treasonable by the law of war.

Foreign residents in an invaded or occupied territory, or foreign visitors in the same, can claim no immunity from this law. They may communicate with foreign parts, or with the inhabitants of the hostile country, so far as the military authority permits, but no further. Instant expulsion from the occupied territory would be the very least punishment for the infraction of this rule.

99.

A messenger carrying written dispatches or verbal messages from one portion of the army, or from a besieged place, to another portion of the same army, or its government, if armed, and in the uniform of his army, and if captured, while doing so, in the territory occupied by the enemy, is treated by the captor as a prisoner of war. If not in uniform, nor a soldier, the circumstances connected with his capture must determine the disposition that shall be made of him.

100.

A messenger or agent who attempts to steal through the territory. occupied by the enemy, to further, in any manner, the interests of the enemy, if captured, is not entitled to the privileges of the prisoner of war, and may be dealt with according to the circumstances of the case.

101.

While deception in war is admitted as a just and necessary means of hostility, and is consistent with honorable warfare, the common law of war allows even capital punishment for clandestine or treacherous attempts to injure an enemy, because they are so dangerous, and it is so difficult to guard against them.

102.

The law of war, like the criminal law regarding other offenses, makes no difference on account of the difference of sexes, concerning the spy, the war-traitor, or the war-rebel.

103.

Spies, war-traitors, and war-rebels are not exchanged according to the common law of war. The exchange of such persons would require a special cartel, authorized by the government, or, at a great distance from it, by the chief commander of the army in the field.

104.

A successful spy or war-traitor, safely returned to his own army, and afterwards captured as an enemy, is not subject to punishment for his acts as a spy or war-traitor, but he may be held in closer custody as a person individually dangerous.

SECTION VI.

Exchange of prisoners—Flags of truce—Flags of protection.

105.

Exchanges of prisoners take place—number for number—rank for rank—wounded for wounded—with added condition for added condition—such, for instance, as not to serve for a certain period.

106.

In exchanging prisoners of war, such numbers of persons of inferior rank may be substituted as an equivalent for one of superior rank as may be agreed upon by cartel, which requires the sanction of the government, or of the commander of the army in the field.

107.

A prisoner of war is in honor bound truly to state to the captor his rank; and he is not to assume a lower rank than belongs to him, in order to cause a more advantageous exchange, nor a higher rank, for the purpose of obtaining better treatment.

Offenses to the contrary have been justly punished by the commanders of released prisoners, and may be good cause for refusing to release such prisoners.

108.

The surplus number of prisoners of war remaining after an exchange has taken place is sometimes released either for the payment of a stipulated sum of money, or, in urgent cases, of provision, clothing, or other necessaries.

Such arrangement, however, requires the sanction of the highest authority.

109.

The exchange of prisoners of war is an act of convenience to both belligerents. If no general cartel has been concluded, it can not be demanded by either of them. No belligerent is obliged to exchange prisoners of war.

A cartel is voidable as soon as either party has violated it.

110.

No exchange of prisoners shall be made except after complete capture, and after an accurate account of them, and a list of the captured officers, has been taken.

111.

The bearer of a flag of truce can not insist upon being admitted. He must always be admitted with great caution. Unnecessary frequency is carefully to be avoided.

112.

If the bearer of a flag of truce offer himself during an engagement, he can be admitted as a very rare exception only. It is no breach of good faith to retain such flag of truce, if admitted during the engagement. Firing is not required to cease on the appearance of a flag of truce in battle.

113.

If the bearer of a flag of truce, presenting himself during an engagement, is killed or wounded, it furnishes no ground of complaint whatever.

114.

If it be discovered, and fairly proved, that a flag of truce has been abused for surreptitiously obtaining military knowledge, the bearer of the flag thus abusing his sacred character is deemed a spy.

So sacred is the character of a flag of truce, and so necessary is its sacredness, that while its abuse is an especially heinous offense, great caution is requisite, on the other hand, in convicting the bearer of a flag of truce as a spy.

115.

It is customary to designate by certain flags (usually yellow) the hospitals in places which are shelled, so that the besieging enemy may avoid firing on them. The same has been done in battles, when hospitals are situated within the field of the engagement.

116.

Honorable belligerents often request that the hospitals within the territory of the enemy may be designated, so that they may be spared.

An honorable belligerent allows himself to be guided by flags or signals of protection as much as the contingencies and the necessities of the fight will permit.

117.

It is justly considered an act of bad faith, of infamy or fiendishness, to deceive the enemy by flags of protection. Such act of bad faith may be good cause for refusing to respect such flags.

118.

The besieging belligerent has sometimes requested the besieged to designate the buildings containing collections of works of art, scientific museums, astronomical observatories, or precious libraries, so that their destruction may be avoided as much as possible.

SECTION VII.

The Parole.

119.

Prisoners of war may be released from captivity by exchange, and, under certain circumstances, also by parole.

120.

The term Parole designates the pledge of individual good faith and honor to do, or to omit doing, certain acts after he who gives his parole shall have been dismissed, wholly or partially, from the power of the captor.

121.

The pledge of the parole is always an individual, but not a private act.

122.

The parole applies chiefly to prisoners of war whom the captor allows to return to their country, or to live in greater freedom within the captor's country or territory, on conditions stated in the parole.

123.

Release of prisoners of war by exchange is the general rule; release by parole is the exception.

124.

Breaking the parole is punished with death when the person breaking the parole is captured again.

Accurate lists, therefore, of the paroled persons must be kept by the belligerents.

125.

When paroles are given and received there must be an exchange of two written documents, in which the name and rank of the paroled individuals are accurately and truthfully stated.

126.

Commissioned officers only are allowed to give their parole, and they can give it only with the permission of their superior, as long as a superior in rank is within reach.

127.

No noncommissioned officer or private can give his parole except through an officer. Individual paroles not given through an officer are not only void, but subject the individuals giving them to the punishment of death as deserters. The only admissible exception is where individuals, properly separated from their commands, have suffered long confinement without the possibility of being paroled through an officer.

128.

No paroling on the battlefield; no paroling of entire bodies of troops after a battle; and no dismissal of large numbers of prisoners, with a general declaration that they are paroled, is permitted, or of any value.

129.

In capitulations for the surrender of strong places or fortified camps the commanding officer, in cases of urgent necessity, may agree that the troops under his command shall not fight again during the war, unless exchanged.

130.

The usual pledge given in the parole is not to serve during the existing war, unless exchanged.

This pledge refers only to the active service in the field, against the paroling belligerent or his allies actively engaged in the same war. These cases of breaking the parole are patent acts, and can be visited with the punishment of death; but the pledge does not refer to internal service, such as recruiting or drilling the recruits, fortifying places not besieged, quelling civil commotions, fighting against belligerents unconnected with the paroling belligerents, or to civil or diplomatic service for which the paroled officer may be employed.

131.

If the government does not approve of the parole, the paroled officer must return into captivity, and should the enemy refuse to receive him, he is free of his parole.

132.

A belligerent government may declare, by a general order, whether it will allow paroling, and on what conditions it will allow it. Such order is communicated to the enemy.

133.

No prisoner of war can be forced by the hostile government to parole himself, and no government is obliged to parole prisoners of war, or to parole all captured officers, if it paroles any. As the pledging of the parole is an individual act, so is paroling, on the other hand, an act of choice on the part of the belligerent.

134.

The commander of an occupying army may require of the civil officers of the enemy, and of its citizens, any pledge he may consider necessary for the safety or security of his army, and upon their failure to give it he may arrest, confine, or detain them.

SECTION VIII.

Armistice—Capitulation.

135.

An armistice is the cessation of active hostilities for a period agreed between belligerents. It must be agreed upon in writing, and duly ratified by the highest authorities of the contending parties.

136.

If an armistice be declared, without conditions, it extends no further than to require a total cessation of hostilities along the front of both belligerents.

If conditions be agreed upon, they should be clearly expressed, and must be rigidly adhered to by both parties. If either party violates any express condition, the armistice may be declared null and void by the other.

137.

An armistice may be general, and valid for all points and lines of the belligerents; or special, that is, referring to certain troops or certain localities only.

An armistice may be concluded for a definite time; or for an indefinite time, during which either belligerent may resume hostilities on giving the notice agreed upon to the other.

138.

The motives which induce the one or the other belligerent to conclude an armistice, whether it be expected to be preliminary to a treaty of peace, or to prepare during the armistice for a more vigorous prosecution of the war, does in no way affect the character of the armistice itself.

139.

An armistice is binding upon the belligerents from the day of the agreed commencement; but the officers of the armies are responsible from the day only when they receive official information of its existence.

140.

Commanding officers have the right to conclude armistices binding on the district over which their command extends, but such armistice is subject to the ratification of the superior authority, and ceases so soon as it is made known to the enemy that the armistice is not ratified, even if a certain time for the elapsing between giving notice of cessation and the resumption of hostilities should have been stipulated for.

141.

It is incumbent upon the contracting parties of an armistice to stipulate what intercourse of persons or traffic between the inhabitants of the territories occupied by the hostile armies shall be allowed, if any.

If nothing is stipulated the intercourse remains suspended, as during actual hostilities.

142.

An armistice is not a partial or a temporary peace; it is only the suspension of military operations to the extent agreed upon by the parties.

143.

When an armistice is concluded between a fortified place and the army besieging it, it is agreed by all the authorities on this subject that the besieger must cease all extension, perfection, or advance of his attacking works as much so as from attacks by main force.

But as there is a difference of opinion among martial jurists, whether the besieged have the right to repair breaches or to erect new works of defense within the place during an armistice, this point should be determined by express agreement between the parties.

144.

So soon as a capitulation is signed, the capitulator has no right to demolish, destroy, or injure the works, arms, stores, or ammunition, in his possession, during the time which elapses between the signing and the execution of the capitulation, unless otherwise stipulated in the same.

145.

When an armistice is clearly broken by one of the parties, the other party is released from all obligation to observe it.

146.

Prisoners taken in the act of breaking an armistice must be treated as prisoners of war, the officer alone being responsible who gives the order for such a violation of an armistice. The highest authority of the belligerent aggrieved may demand redress for the infraction of an armistice.

147.

Belligerents sometimes conclude an armistice while their plenipotentiaries are met to discuss the conditions of a treaty of peace; but plenipotentiaries may meet without a preliminary armistice; in the latter case, the war is carried on without any abatement.

SECTION IX.

Assassination.

148.

The law of war does not allow proclaiming either an individual belonging to the hostile army, or a citizen, or a subject of the hostile government, an outlaw, who may be slain without trial by any captor, any more than the modern law of peace allows such intentional outlawry; on the contrary, it abhors such outrage. The sternest retaliation should follow the murder committed in consequence of such proclamation, made by whatever authority. Civilized nations look with horror upon offers of rewards for the assassination of enemies as relapses into barbarism.

SECTION X.

Insurrection—Civil War—Rebellion.

149.

Insurrection is the rising of people in arms against their government, or a portion of it, or against one or more of its laws, or against an officer or officers of the government. It may be confined to mere armed resistance, or it may have greater ends in view.

150.

Civil war is war between two or more portions of a country or state, each contending for the mastery of the whole, and each claiming to be the legitimate government. The term is also sometimes applied to war of rebellion, when the rebellious provinces or portions of the state are contiguous to those containing the seat of government.

151.

The term rebellion is applied to an insurrection of large extent, and is usually a war between the legitimate government of a country and portions of provinces of the same who seek to throw off their allegiance to it and set up a government of their own.

152.

When humanity induces the adoption of the rules of regular war toward rebels, whether the adoption is partial or entire, it does in no way whatever imply a partial or complete acknowledgment of their government, if they have set up one, or of them, as an independent and sovereign power. Neutrals have no right to make the adoption of the rules of war by the assailed government toward rebels the ground of their own acknowledgment of the revolted people as an independent power.

153.

Treating captured rebels as prisoners of war, exchanging them, concluding of cartels, capitulations, or other warlike agreements with them; addressing officers of a rebel army by the rank they may have in the same; accepting flags of truce; or, on the other hand, proclaiming martial law in their territory, or levying war-taxes or forced loans, or doing any other act sanctioned or demanded by the law and usages of public war between sovereign belligerents, neither proves nor establishes an acknowledgment of the rebellious people, or of the government which they may have erected, as a public or sovereign power. Nor does the adoption of the rules of war toward rebels imply an engagement with them extending beyond the limits of these rules. It is victory in the field that ends the strife and settles the future relations between the contending parties.

154.

Treating, in the field, the rebellious enemy according to the law and usages of war has never prevented the legitimate government from trying the leaders of the rebellion or chief rebels for high treason, and from treating them accordingly, unless they are included in a general amnesty.

155.

All enemies in regular war are divided into two general classes—that is to say, into combatants and noncombatants, or unarmed citizens of the hostile government.

The military commander of the legitimate government, in a war of rebellion, distinguishes between the loyal citizen in the revolted portion of the country and the disloyal citizen. The disloyal citizens may further be classified into those citizens known to sympathize with the rebellion without positively aiding it, and those who, without taking up arms, give positive aid and comfort to the rebellious enemy without being bodily forced thereto.

156.

Common justice and plain expediency require that the military commander protect the manifestly loyal citizens, in revolted territories, against the hardships of the war as much as the common misfortune of all war admits.

The commander will throw the burden of the war, as much as lies within his power, on the disloyal citizens, of the revolted portion or province, subjecting them to a stricter police than the noncombatant enemies have to suffer in regular war; and if he deems it appropriate, or if his government demands of him that every citizen shall, by an oath of allegiance, or by some other manifest act, declare his fidelity to the legitimate government, he may expel, transfer, imprison, or fine the revolted citizens who refuse to pledge themselves anew as citizens obedient to the law and loyal to the government.

Whether it is expedient to do so, and whether reliance can be placed upon such oaths, the commander or his government have the right to decide.

157.

Armed or unarmed resistance by citizens of the United States against the lawful movements of their troops is levying war against the United States, and is therefore treason.

INDEX.

GUERRILLA PARTIES

CONSIDERED WITH REFERENCE TO THE

LAWS AND USAGES OF WAR.

WRITTEN AT THE REQUEST OF

MAJOR-GENERAL HENRY W. HALLECK,

GENERAL-IN-CHIEF OF THE ARMY OF THE UNITED STATES.

War has its laws and justice, as well as Peace, and we have learned to make war justly, no less than bravely.—*Camillus*, in LIVY V., 27.

BY

FRANCIS LIEBER,

IN THE MONTH OF AUGUST, 1862.

ORDERED BY THE DEPARTMENT OF WAR TO BE PRINTED FOR DISTRIBUTION IN THE ARMY.

NEW YORK.

D. VAN NOSTRAND, 192 BROADWAY.

1862.

BAKER & GODWIN, PRINTERS,
Printing-House Square, opposite City Hall
NEW YORK.

LETTER

OF

MAJOR-GENERAL H. W. HALLECK

TO

FRANCIS LIEBER.

HEADQUARTERS OF THE ARMY,
Washington, Aug. 6, 1862.

DR. FRANCIS LIEBER, New York.

My dear Doctor :—Having heard that you have given much attention to the usages and customs of war as practiced in the present
age, and especially to the matter of guerrilla war, I hope you may
find it convenient to give to the public your views on that subject.
The rebel authorities claim the right to send men, in the garb of
peaceful citizens, to waylay and attack our troops, to burn bridges
and houses, and to destroy property and persons within our lines.
They demand that such persons be treated as ordinary belligerents,
and that when captured they have extended to them the same rights
as other prisoners of war; they also threaten that if such persons
be punished as marauders and spies, they will retaliate by executing
our prisoners of war in their possession.

I particularly request your views on these questions.

Very respectfully,

Your obedient servant,

H. W. HALLECK,

General-in-Chief U. S. A.

ERRATA.

Page 12, line 20, *read* which *for* who.
" 16, " 10, *omit* as.
" " " 12, *read* last century and *for* war just mentioned, so new.
" " " 13, *add* is new *after* war.
" 17, " 21, *read* picket *for* speaking.
" 20, " 25, *add* not *after* does.

GUERRILLA PARTIES

CONSIDERED WITH REFERENCE TO THE

LAWS AND USAGES OF WAR.

THE position of armed parties loosely attached to the main body of the army, or altogether unconnected with it, has rarely been taken up by writers on the law of war. The term Guerrilla is often inaccurately used, and its application has been particularly confused at the present time. From these circumstances arises much of the difficulty which presents itself to the publicist and martial jurist in treating of guerrilla parties. The subject is substantially a new topic in the law of war, and it is besides exposed to the mischievous process, so often employed in our day, of throwing the mantle of a novel term around an old and well-known offence, in the expectation that a legalizing effect will result from the adoption of a new word having a technical sound; an illustration of which occurred in the introduction of the Latin and rarer term Repudiation to designate the old practice of dishonestly declining the payment of debts—an offence with which the world has been acquainted ever since men united in the bonds of society. We find that self-constituted bands in the South, who destroy the cotton stored by their own neighbors, are styled in the journals of the North as well as in those of the South, Guerrillas; while in truth they are, according to the common law— not of war only, but that of every society—simply armed robbers, against whom every person is permitted, or is in duty bound, to use all the means of defence at his disposal; as, in a late instance, even General Toombs of Georgia, declared to a certain committee of safety of his State, that he would defend the planting and producing of his cotton; though, I must own, *he* did not call the self-constituted committee *Guerrillas*, but, if memory serves me right, Scoundrels.

The term Guerrilla is the diminutive of the Spanish word *guerra*, war, and means petty war, that is war carried on by detached parties; generally in the mountains. It means, farther, the party of men united under one chief engaged in petty war, which, in the eastern portion of Europe and the whole Levant, is called a *capitanery*, a band under one capitano. The term *Guerrilla*, however, is not applied in Spain to a single man of the party; such a person is called *Guerillero*, or more frequently *Partida*, which means partisan. Thus Napier, in speaking of the guerrilla, in his History of the Peninsular War, uses, with rare exception, the term Partidas for the chiefs and men engaged in the petty war against the French. It is worthy of notice that the dictionary of the Spanish academy gives, as the first meaning of the word *Guerrilla* —"A party of light troops for reconnoissance, and opening the first skirmishes." I translate from an edition of 1826, published, therefore, long after the Peninsular War, through which the term Guerrilla has passed over into many other European languages. Self-constitution is not

a necessary element of the meaning given by the Spaniards or by many writers of other nations to the word
Guerrilla, although it is true that the guerrilla parties in
the Peninsular War were nearly all self-constituted, since
the old government had been destroyed; and the forces
which had been called into existence by the provisional
government, were no more acknowledged by the French
as regular troops, than the self-constituted bands under
leading priests, lawyers, smugglers, or peasants: because
the French did not acknowledge the provisional Junta or
Cortes. Many of the guerrilleros were shot when made
prisoners; as the guerrilla chiefs executed French prisoners
in turn. It is the state of things these bands almost always lead to, according to their inherent character; yet,
when the *partidas* of Mina and Empecinado had swelled
to the imposing number of twenty thousand and more,
which fact of itself implies a certain degree of discipline,
Mina made a regular treaty with the French for the passage of certain French goods through the lines, and on
these the partisan leader levied regular duties according
to a tariff agreed upon between the belligerents arrayed
against one another in fierce hostility.

What, then, do we in the present time understand by
the word Guerrilla? In order to ascertain the law or to
settle it according to elements already existing, it will be
necessary ultimately to give a distinct definition; but it
may be stated here that whatever may be our final definition, it is universally understood in this country at the
present time that a guerrilla party means an irregular
band of armed men, carrying on an irregular war, not
being able, according to their character as a guerrilla
party, to carry on what the law terms a *regular* war.
The irregularity of the guerrilla party consists in its ori-

gin, for it is either self-constituted or constituted by the call of a single individual, not according to the general law of levy, conscription, or volunteering; it consists in its disconnection with the army, as to its pay, provision, and movements, and it is irregular as to the permanency of the band, which may be dismissed and called again together at any time. These are, I believe, constituent ideas of the term Guerrilla as now used. Other ideas are associated with the term, differently by different persons. Thus, many persons associate the idea of pillage with the guerrilla band, because, not being connected with the regular army, the men cannot provide for themselves, except by pillage, even in their own country—acts of violence with which the Spanish guerrilleros sorely afflicted their own countrymen in the Peninsular War. Others connect with it the idea of intentional destruction for the sake of destruction, because the guerrilla chief cannot aim at any strategic advantages or any regular fruits of victory. Others, again, associate with it the idea of the danger with which the spy surrounds us, because he that to-day passes you in the garb and mien of a peaceful citizen, may to-morrow, as a guerrilla man, fire your house or murder you from behind the hedge. Others connect with the guerrillero the idea of necessitated murder, because guerrilla bands cannot encumber themselves with prisoners of war; they have, therefore, frequently, perhaps generally, killed their prisoners, and of course have been killed in turn when made prisoners, thus introducing a system of barbarity which becomes intenser in its demoralization as it spreads and is prolonged. Others, again, connect the ideas of general and heinous criminality, of robbery and lust with the term, because the organization of the party being but slight and the leader utterly dependent upon the band, little discipline can be enforced, and where no discipline is enforced in war a state of things results which resembles far more the wars recorded in Froissart or Comines, or the Thirty Years' War, and the Religious War in France, than the regular wars of modern times. And such a state of things results speedily too; for all growth, progress and rearing, moral or material, are slow; all destruction, relapse and degeneracy, fearfully rapid. It requires the power of the Almighty and a whole century to grow an oak tree; but only a pair of arms, an ax and an hour or two, to cut it down.

History confirms these associations, but the law of war as well as the law of peace has treated many of these and kindred subjects,—acts justifiable, offensive, or criminal,—under acknowledged terms, namely: the Freebooter, the Marauder, the Brigand, the Partisan, the Free-corps, the Spy, the Rebel, the Conspirator, the Robber, and especially the Highway Robber, the Rising en Masse, or the "Arming of Peasants."

A few words on some of these subjects will aid us in coming to a clearer understanding of the main topic which occupies our attention.

Freebooter is a term which was in common use in the English language at no very remote period; it is of rare use now, because the freebooter makes his appearance but rarely in modern times, thanks to the more regular and efficient governments, and to the more advanced state of the law of war. From the freebooter at sea arose the privateer, for the privateer is a commissioned freebooter, or the freebooter taken into the service of the government by the letter of marque. The Sea-Gueux, in the Revolution of the Netherlands, were originally freebooters at

1*

sea, and they were always treated, when captured, simply as freebooters. Wherever the freebooter is taken, at sea or on land, death is inflicted upon him now as in former times; for freebooters are nothing less than armed robbers of the most dangerous and criminal type, banded together for the purposes of booty and of common protection.

The Brigand is, in military language, the soldier who detaches himself from his troop and commits robbery, naturally accompanied in many cases with murder and other crimes of violence. His punishment, inflicted even by his own authorities, is death. The word Brigand, derived as it is from *briguer*, to beg, meant originally beggar, but it soon came to be applied to armed strollers, a class of men which swarmed in all countries in the middle ages. The term has, however, received a wider meaning in modern military terminology. He that assails the enemy without or against the authority of his own government, is called, even though his object should be wholly free from any intention of pillage, a brigand, subject to the infliction of death, if captured. When Major von Schill, commanding a Prussian regiment of huzzars, marched, in the year 1809, against the French, without the order of his government, for the purpose of causing a rising of the people in the North of Germany, while Napoleon was occupied in the South with Austria, Schill was declared by Napoleon and his brother, *a brigand*, and the King of Westphalia, Jerome Bonaparte, offered a reward of ten thousand francs for his head. Schill was killed in battle; but twelve young officers of his troop, taken prisoners, were carried by the French to the fortress Wesel, where a court-martial declared them prisoners of war. Napoleon quashed the finding, ordered a new court-martial, and they were all shot as brigands. Napoleon is not cited here as an authority in the law of war; he and many of his Generals frequently substituted the harshest violence for martial usages. The case is mentioned as an illustration of the meaning attached to the word Brigand in the Law of War, and of the fact that death is the acknowledged punishment for the brigand.

The terms Partisan and Free-corps are vaguely used. Sometimes, as we shall see farther on, partisan is used for a self-constituted *guerrillero ;* more frequently it has a different meaning. Both partisan-corps and free-corps designate bodies detached from the main army ; but the former term refers to the action of the troop, the latter to the composition. The partisan leader commands a corps whose object is to injure the enemy by action separate from that of his own main army ; the partisan acts chiefly upon the enemy's lines of connection and communication, and outside of or beyond the lines of operation of his own army, in the rear and on the flanks of the enemy. Rapid and varying movements and surprises are the chief means of his success ; but he is part and parcel of the army, and, as such, considered entitled to the privileges of the law of war, so long as he does not transgress it. Free-corps, on the other hand, are troops not belonging to the regular army, consisting of volunteers, generally raised by individuals authorized to do so by the government, used for petty war, and not incorporated with the *Ordre de bataille.* They were known in the middle ages. The French *compagnies franches* were free-corps ; but this latter term came into use only in the 18th century. They were generally in bad repute, given to pillage and other excesses ; but this is incidental. There were many free-corps in Germany opposed to Napoleon, when that country rose against the French, but the men composing them were entitled to the benefits of the law of war, and generally received them when taken prisoner. These free-corps were composed, in many cases, of high-minded patriots. The difficulty regarding free-corps and partisans arises from the fact that their discipline is often lax, and used to be so especially in the last century, so that frequently they cannot cumber themselves with prisoners; and that, even for their own support, they are often obliged to pillage or to extort money from the places they occupy. They are treated, therefore, according to their deserts, on the principle of retaliation; but there is nothing inherently lawless or brigand-like in their character.

The Spy, the Rebel, and Conspirator deserve notice in this place simply with reference to persons acting as such, and belonging to the population of the country or district occupied by a hostile force. A person dwelling in a district under military occupation, and giving information to the government of which he was subject, but who has been expelled by the victorious invader, is universally treated as a spy—a spy of a peculiarly dangerous character. The most patriotic motives would not shield such a person from the doom of the spy. There have been high-minded and self-sacrificing spies, but, when captured, even if belonging to the armies themselves, they have never been treated otherwise than as common spies. Even mere secret correspondence of a person in an occupied district with the enemy, though the contents of the correspondence may have been innocent, has subjected the correspondent to serious consequences, and sometimes to the rigor of martial law, especially if the offence be committed after a proclamation to the contrary. Prince

Hatzfeld was appointed by the King of Prussia, on his leaving the capital after the battle of Jena, to conduct public affairs in Berlin, until the city should be occupied by the French, and to send a report to the King every morning until the occupation by the enemy should have taken place. Prince Hatzfeld sent such a report to his own government, giving the number of the French who had arrived at Potzdam on the 24th of October, at 5 o'clock A. M.—that is, seven hours before the French vanguard entered Berlin. The letter fell into the hands of Napoleon. It is well known that the Emperor, at the supplication of the Princess, allowed her husband to escape the penalty of a spy. Whatever may be thought of the question, whether the Prince, by sending the letter at the hour mentioned, became a spy or not, no one has ever doubted that, had he secretly corresponded with his government after the occupation of Berlin by the French, giving information of the occupants, the French would have been justified in treating him as a spy. The spy becomes, in this case, peculiarly dangerous, making hostile use of the protection which, by the modern law of war, the victor extends to the persons and property of the conquered. Similar remarks apply to the rebel, taking the word in the primitive meaning of *rebellare*—that is, to return to war after having been conquered ; and to conspiracies—that is, secret agreements leading to such resumption of arms in bands of whatever number, or, which is still worse, plans to murder from secret places.

This war-rebel, as we might term him, this renewer of war within an occupied territory, has been universally treated with the utmost rigor of the military law. The war-rebel exposes the occupying army to the greatest danger, and essentially interferes with the mitigation of the severity of war, which it is one of the noblest objects of the modern law of war to obtain. Whether the war-rebel rises on his own account, or whether he has been secretly called upon by his former government to do so, would make no difference whatever. The royalists who recently rose in the mountains of Calabria against the national government of Italy, and in favor of Francis, who had been their king until within a recent period, were treated as brigands and shot, unless, indeed, pardoned on prudential grounds.

The rising *en masse*, or "the arming of peasants," as it used to be called, brings us nearer to the subject of the guerrilla parties. Down to the beginning of the first French revolution, toward the end of last century, the spirit which pervaded all governments of the European continent was, that the people were rather the passive substratum of the State than an essential portion of it. The governments were considered to be the State; wars were chiefly cabinet wars, not national wars—not the people's affairs.

Moser, in his Contributions to the latest European Law of Nations in Times of War (a German work, in 3 vols., from 1779–1781), gives remarkable instances of the claims which the conqueror was believed to have on the property and on the subjects of the hostile country. They were believed to be of so extensive a character that the French, when in Germany, during the seven years' war, literally drafted Germans for the French army, and used them as their own soldiers—although, it must be added, that loud complaints were made, and the French felt themselves obliged to make some sort of explanation. The same work contains instances of complaints being made against arming the peasants, or of levies *en masse*,

as contrary to the law of nations; but Moser also shows
that the Austrians employed the Tyrolese (always familiar
with the use of the rifle) in war, without any complaint of
the adversary.

Since that time most constitutions contain provisions
that the people have a right to possess and use arms;
everywhere *national* armies have been introduced, and
the military law of many countries puts arms into the
hands of all. Austria armed the people, as militia, in
1805; Russia, in 1812; and Prussia introduced the most
comprehensive measure of arming the people in 1813.
The militia proper was called *Landwehr*; and those who
were too old for service in the Landwehr were intended
to form the *Landsturm*—citizens armed as well as the
circumstances might permit, and to be used for whatever
military service within their own province they might be
found fit. It is true that the French threatened to treat
them as brigands—that is to say, not to treat them as
prisoners of war if captured. The French, however, were
expelled from Germany, and no opportunity was given to
test their threat.

I believe it can be said that the most recent publicists
and writers on international law agree that the rising of
the people to repel invasion entitles them to the full benefits of the law of war, and that the invader cannot well
inquire into the origin of the armed masses opposing him;
that is to say, he will be obliged to treat the captured
citizens in arms as prisoners of war, so long as they
openly oppose him in respectable numbers, and have risen
in the yet uninvaded or unconquered portions of the hostile country.

Their acting in separate bodies does not necessarily
give them a different character. Some entire wars have

been carried on by separate bands or capitaneries, such as the recent war of independence of Greece. It is true, indeed, that the question of the treatment of prisoners was not discussed in that war, because the Turkish Government killed or enslaved all prisoners; but I take it that a civilized government would not have allowed the fact that the Greeks fought in detached parties and carried on mountain guerrilla to influence its conduct toward prisoners.

I may here observe that, as the question how captured guerrilleros ought to be treated was not much discussed in the war just mentioned, so new, comparatively, is the whole discussion in the law of war. This will not surprise us when we consider that so justly celebrated a publicist as Bynkershoeck defended, as late as the beginning of last century, the killing of common prisoners of war.

It does not seem that, in the case of a rising *en masse*, the absence of a uniform can constitute a difference. There are cases, indeed, in which the absence of a uniform may be taken as very serious *prima facie* evidence against an armed prowler or marauder, but it must be remembered that a uniform dress is a matter of impossibility in a levy *en masse;* and in some cases regulars have had no uniforms, at least for a considerable time. The Southern prisoners made at Fort Donelson, whom I have seen at the West, had no uniform. They were indeed dressed very much alike, but it was the uniform dress of the countryman in that region. Yet they were treated by us as prisoners of war, and well treated too. Nor would it be difficult to adopt something of a badge, easily put on and off, and to call it a uniform. It makes a great difference, however, whether the absence of the uniform is used for the purpose of concealment or disguise, in order to get by stealth within the lines of the invader, for destruction of life or property, or for pillage, and whether the parties have no organization at all, and are so small that they cannot act otherwise than by stealth. Nor can it be maintained in good faith, or with any respect for sound sense and judgment, that an individual—an armed prowler—(now frequently called a bushwhacker) shall be entitled to the protection of the law of war, simply because he says that he has taken up his gun in defence of his country, or because his government or his chief has issued a proclamation by which he calls upon the people to infest the bushes and commit homicides which every civilized nation will consider murders. Indeed, the importance of writing on this subject is much diminished by the fact that the soldier generally decides these cases for himself. The most disciplined soldiers will execute on the spot an armed and murderous prowler found where he could have no business as a peaceful citizen. Even an enemy in the uniform of the hostile army would stand little chance of protection, if found prowling near the opposing army, separate from his own troops at a greater than speaking distance, and under generally suspicious circumstances. The chance would, of course, be far less if the prowler is in the common dress worn by the countryman of the district. It may be added here, that a person proved to be a regular soldier of the enemy's army, found in citizens' dress within the lines of the captor, is universally dealt with as a spy.

It has been stated, that the word Guerrilla is not only used for individuals engaged in petty war, but frequently as an equivalent of partisan. General Halleck, in his International Law, or Rules regulating the Intercourse of States in Peace and War, San Francisco, 1861, page 386, and seq., seems to consider partisan troops and guerrilla troops as the same, and seems to consider "self-constitution" a characteristic of the partisan; while other legal and military writers define partisan as I have stated, namely, a soldier belonging to a corps which operates in the manner given above. I beg the reader to peruse that passage, both on account of its own value and of the many important and instructive authorities which he will find there. They are collected with that careful industry which distinguishes the whole work.

Dr. T. D. Woolsey, page 299, seq., of his Introduction to the Study of International Law, Boston, 1860, says: "The treatment which the milder modern usage prescribes for regular soldiers is extended also to militia called out by public authority. Guerrilla parties, however, do not enjoy the full benefit of the laws of war. They are apt to fare worse than either regular troops or an armed peasantry. The reasons for this are, that they are annoying and insidious, that they put on and off with ease the character of a soldier, and that they are prone, themselves, to treat their enemies who fall into their hands with great severity."

If the term partisan is used in the sense in which I have defined it, it is not necessary to treat of it specially. The partisan, in this sense, is, of course, answerable for the commission of those acts to which the law of war grants no protection, and by which the soldier forfeits being treated as a prisoner of war, if captured.

It is different, if we understand by guerrilla parties, self-constituted sets of armed men, in times of war, who form no integrant part of the organized army, do not stand on the regular pay-roll of the army, or are not paid at all, take up arms and lay them down at intervals, and carry on petty war (guerrilla) chiefly by raids, extortion, destruction, and massacre, and who cannot encumber themselves with many prisoners, and will therefore generally give no quarter.

They are peculiarly dangerous, because they easily evade pursuit, and by laying down their arms become insidious enemies; because they cannot otherwise subsist than by rapine, and almost always degenerate into simple robbers or brigands. The Spanish guerrilla bands against Napoleon proved a scourge to their own countrymen, and became efficient for their own cause only in the same degree in which they gradually became disciplined. The royalists in the north of France, during the first Revolution, although setting out with sentiments of loyal devotion to their unfortunate king, soon degenerated into bands of robbers, while many robbers either joined them or assumed the name of royalists. Napoleon states that their brigandage gave much trouble, and obliged the Government to resort to the severest measures.

For an account of the misdeeds and want of efficiency of the Spanish guerrilleros, the reader is referred to Napier's Peninsular War, and especially to Chapter II., Book XVII.; while he will find, in Guizot's Memoirs, Vol. IV., page 100, seq., that in the struggle between the Christinos and Carlists, the guerrilla parties under Mina and Zumalacarreguy, regularly massacred their mutual prisoners, until the evil became so revolting to the Spaniards themselves that a regular treaty was concluded between the parties, stipulating the exchange of prisoners immediately after being made. How the surplus on the one or the other side was dealt with, I do not know; but the treaty, concluded after the butchering of prisoners had been going on for a long time, is mentioned in all the histories of that period.

But when guerrilla parties aid the main army of a belligerent, it will be difficult for the captor of guerrilla-men to decide at once whether they are regular partisans, distinctly authorized by their own government; and it would seem that we are borne out by the conduct of the most humane belligerents in recent times, and by many of the modern writers, if the rule be laid down, that guerrilla-men, when captured in fair fight and open warfare, should be treated as the regular partisan is, until special crimes, such as murder, or the killing of prisoners, or the sacking of places, are proved upon them; leaving the question of self-constitution unexamined.

. The law of war, however, would not extend a similar favor to small bodies of armed country people, near the lines, whose very smallness shows that they must resort to occasional fighting and the occasional assuming of peaceful habits, and to brigandage. The law of war would still less favor them when they trespass within the hostile lines to commit devastation, rapine, or destruction. Every European army has treated such persons, and it seems to me would continue, even in the improved state of the present usages of war, to treat them as brigands, whatever prudential mercy might decide upon in single cases. This latter consideration cannot be discussed here; it does appertain to the law of war.

It has been stated already, that the armed prowler, the so-called bushwhacker, is a simple assassin, and will thus always be considered by soldier and citizen; and we have likewise seen that the armed bands that rise in a district fairly occupied by military force, or in the rear of an army, are universally considered, if captured, brigands, and not prisoners of war. They unite the fourfold character of the spy, the brigand, the assassin, and the rebel, and cannot—indeed, it must be supposed, will not—expect to be treated as a fair enemy of the regular war. They know what a hazardous career they enter upon when they take up arms, and that, were the case reversed, they would surely not grant the privileges of regular warfare to persons who should thus rise in their rear.

I have thus endeavored to ascertain what may be considered the law of war, or fair rules of action toward so-called guerrilla parties. I do not enter upon a consideration of their application to the civil war in which we are engaged, nor of the remarkable claims recently set up by our enemies, demanding us to act according to certain rules which they have signally and officially disregarded toward us. I have simply proposed to myself to find a certain portion of the law of war. The application of the laws and usages of war to wars of insurrection or rebellion, is always undefined, and depends upon relaxations of the municipal law, suggested by humanity or necessitated by the numbers engaged in the insurrection. The law of war, as acknowledged between independent belligerents, is, at times, not allowed to interfere with the municipal law of rebellion, or is allowed to do so only very partially, as was the case in Great Britain during the Stuart rebellion, in the middle of last century ; at other times, again, measures are adopted in rebellions, by the victorious party or the legitimate government, more lenient even than the international law of war. Neither of these topics can occupy us here, nor does the letter prefixed to this tract contain the request that I should do so. How far rules which have formed themselves in the course of time between belligerents might be relaxed, with safety, toward the evil-doers in our civil war, or how far such relaxation or mitigation would be likely to produce a bene-

ficial effect upon an enemy who in committing a great and
bewildering Wrong seems to have withdrawn himself from
the common influences of fairness, sympathy, truth, and
logic—how far this ought to be done, at the present mo-
ment, must be decided by the executive power, civil and
military, or possibly by the legislative power. It is not for
me, in this place, to make the inquiry. So much is certain,
that no army, no society, engaged in war, any more than a
society at peace, can allow unpunished assassination, robbery, and devastation, without the deepest injury to itself
and disastrous consequences, which might change the very
issue of the war.

www.ingramcontent.com/pod-product-compliance
Lightning Source LLC
Chambersburg PA
CBHW021347090426
42742CB00008B/767